Praise for Richard Hoffman's poetry:

We need more writers like Richard Hoffman who still consider poetry a force for change and the greater good, and a balm to human suffering. His poems do not dazzle, are not overly self-conscious and don't seek incandescent effects. A poet of the Rust Belt, Hoffman is, like his own steelworker father, a worker among workers, full of common sense, with a fine sense of the workable and the doable. His poems are as practical as a lunch bucket or a steel helmet. What impresses are his psychological insights, both in prose and poetry, and his philosophical musings, which come from living in the world.

> — **M.G. Stephens,** writing in *PN Review* (U.K.)

If Anton Chekhov returned as a modern-day poet, Richard Hoffman would be his name. His poems reverberate with the same lucid witness and precision. Bridging histories local and cultural, they draw on literary traditions while simultaneously heralding experiment and invention.

> — **Terrance Hayes,** author of *American Sonnets for My Past and Future Assassin*

Richard Hoffman is a fiercely gifted poet whose stanzas revel in the infinite possibilities of language, and jolt, surprise, and satisfy at every turn. This is work to be savored and embraced.

> — **Patricia Smith,** author of *The Intentions of Thunder: New & Selected Poems*

Hoffman taps into moments when civilization dissolves, not superficially, but at its emotional roots. Time and again through the poet's weary irony comes the bite of life.

> — **Molly Peacock,** author of *The Widow's Crayon Box*

Beautiful and dangerous, unforgettable, transformational, meaningful across academic and social borders.

> — **Linda McCarriston,** author of *Eva-Mary*

Hoffman is a rarity; his premise is dialogic, his canvas vast, his stance self-questioning. This new book is breakthrough work of hard-earned grounding, profound integrity, and scalding, visionary intensity.
   — **D. Nurkse,** author of *A Country of Strangers: New &*
      Selected Poems

Hoffman is the poet traveling our nightmare of now, our descent into a lack of love for one another, but along the way he finds etchings of hope on the walls amid all the signs of a falling away from a center that has forgotten how to hold. Hoffman's tropes and incantations invite us to shed a wisdom that has grown archaic so that we can begin to reclaim the genuine and live.
   — **Afaa Michael Weaver,** author of *A Fire in the Hills*

People Once Real redefines elegy. Elegy for the present of our failing democracy, our failing planet, our failing bodies. Elegy for the futures we had imagined would be. Elegy for the past of our forgotten lessons, for our dead that we must praise or forgive to finally let some part of ourselves die. Elegy for the self that ultimately leads Hoffman toward the grace of love that saves us all from emotional oblivion. William Blake meets Walt Whitman in Hoffman, a voice of unparalleled lyricism that is both utterly intimate and specific, as it is wisely oracular and mystical, with a density of breathtaking metaphors that truly elucidate the life and death, death and life of all things that matter in our lives.
   — **Richard Blanco,** 2013 Presidential Inaugural Poet, author of
      Homeland of My Body: New & Selected Poems

Hoffman is a moral poet, not some hectoring, vengeful, finger-pointing after-the-fact moralist, but one fully engaged in our living moment who wants us to be better, to curb what he calls our "capricious hungers" because they have costs, obvious or hidden, and what is being done for our appetites or in our name is our responsibility... Hoffman's poems scare, inspire, and comfort. They're generous, insistent, and beautiful in the way that only truth can be.
   — **Rick Larios,** writing in *The Manhattan Review*

Each Child a Disappearance

New and Selected Poems, 1972-2025

Richard Hoffman

LILY POETRY REVIEW BOOKS

Copyright © 2026 by Richard Hoffman
Published by Lily Poetry Review Books
223 Winter Street
Whitman, MA 02382

https://lilypoetryreview.blog/

ISBN: 978-1-957755-72-4

Cover art: Detail, *Abduction of Ganymede* by Rembrandt van Rijn

Table of Contents

Yet

Sounds East European, doesn't it?
Yet.
A town in the Urals, the western
border of Asia, where everyone hurries
calmly through the narrowest of streets
to rocky fields, hard, patched by snow so dry
it hurts. Yet
every single day they make their way there;
every night come back.

The ring of an ancient Egyptian god.
An animal, probably like a musk-ox,
slowly dragging tomorrow from over the mountains;
(can a word be a god? can anything but
a word be a god? for us, I mean)
always and never arriving.

Umbilicus: Vision: Promise: Deadlock:
(the deciding vote has not been cast
yet) I, pharoah by default, acknowledge you
most powerful of all. O lord of heads sometimes,
tails sometimes, lord of the other hand,
there is no escape from you
yet.

After a Death

Never so empty as in that hour just after
        my wailing grief at the news,
I swear I could hear the moon's wet tires
        on its smooth road through the clouds,
and could hear the thin clouds shifting, too,
        crossing the clear constellations.
So I drove far out in the country,
        deep in the dark on a road through a field
and stopped and climbed up on the roof of the car
        and lay there beneath such magnificence
I thought I'd left the earth.

Rune

A day nears, feast
of a saint unborn,
unlike our forebears'
or any we have known.

We know how dark
are powers kept in darkness
(a broken lock, a stopped clock,
masks, and lies.)

When we wake
that unexampled day,
will we believe ourselves
free or broken?

Upon a Time

There must once have been a world
      where, seeing the destruction of a school,
            I would think *earthquake*, not *airstrike*.

Where rubble, twisted rebar, and broken
      aggregate did not become a place
            for children to hide from soldiers.

Where seeing a photo of a child's corpse,
      a broken tiny body of no one's ancestor,
            I would not wonder if, her bones now free

to be bone, to grow brittle, dull, hollow,
      and apolitical in the ancient land of her birth
and death, she is not better off.

Diaspora (Monster)

Someone must have summoned the ancestors,
decided only they could help us out of this one,
because here she comes, irascible and urgent, great

great grandmother, saying *Make way, make way!*
in a language only a few here understand.
Although she is terrified, she is willing as ever

to fish you from the pond, post bail, make soup,
even, this time, suffer ridicule and learn
to settle for canned hilarity, eat freeze-dried

produce if that's what it takes; for love of you,
to register at PROGRESS BARGAIN DRIVING SCHOOL
and take the test and drive across deserts

and borders just to find you tangled in your plans,
regrets, and terrors in the city of tomorrow,
everywhere under construction, wooden barricades,

orange DETOUR signs proliferating and compounding
the affront and officious dismissal of one-way streets.
Even now she is stuck in the cross-town jam of

your jackhammered consciousness's flying sparks,
muttering *I'm coming, I'm coming.* See her there?
Do something. Wave your arms. *Over here, over here!*

Whoever You Are

In every age are two people
charged with holding up the sky.

Those who know them know
something's different about them.

Usually, the two do not meet;
however, sometimes, after eons,

the law of averages requires
they collide, transforming both.

Those two were your parents.
But you knew that, didn't you?

A Face in the Ceiling

In August heat, I am remembering my father.
"Stinkin' hot," he would have called this day,
his T-shirt wet with sweat over his heart, wet
circles under his arms, dark patch between his
shoulder blades. I am remembering my father,
a year now since his death has scattered him,
no longer all in one place anymore, no longer
in one time. Now, piecing him back together

near the anniversary of his dissolution,
questions — not coming from me, not curiosity
but necessity (mine and his together) — form
in the discontinuous and widening vacancies
of memory, questions like sweat, beading
on my forehead. This is work, not to let him go,
not yet, and to ask if I have understood him;
hazardous work. I am remembering my father

as he was in my earliest memories, home
from "the steel" where he laid track in the yards,
sprawled on the floor of the living room, spent,
in his boxer shorts in front of an oscillating fan
that dinged at intervals at some point in its sweep
(I swear I can hear it now. I can hear it!).
I lay next to him, and he asked if I could see
the faces in the cracked and water-stained ceiling.

Yes. I saw them there. Who were they? But
by then he was asleep, so I pretended I was too.
One time at least, I was. Some years later, home
from his job with the city, ("Those years," he'd say,
"I was with the city") a restaurant inspector,

("protecting the public," he'd say and roll his eyes)
in the same blue uniform as a cop, without the gun,
I spied on him searching his face in the mirror.

For what? For whom? I am remembering my father
with the help of photographs and a single video
in which he says how good it feels to tell the truth.
You have to think of a man in time, even a father.
I think of him as a man on whom lies were heaped
until he could hardly breathe. I think that goodness
prior to injury is innocence, and that goodness after
injury is courage. I am remembering my father.

Watching

Because I lay on my back as a boy
in the grass of the small yard behind our house

      watching clouds move and become
                  faces, mostly,

I was able to sit for a long time
      holding my dying mother's hand
           as her sleeping face changed
     like a field in the sun
under drifting
              clouds,

and hold my newborn grandson,
     his features changing
moment to moment,
           affected by something
     perhaps like dreaming

at which I wonder.

The Scientific Method

When you begin to feel the first tear well,
place the vial against the lower lid and,
gently, with the fingers of your other hand,
lift above the eye. Let the tear fall

by itself - don't touch it - in the vial.
It helps to do this in front of a mirror.
Remember: be honest if you make an error.
Naturalness and purity are essential.

Keep at least that one eye open wide.
Don't force the tear in any way.
Sometimes a tear won't come on a given day.
Make note of the fact that you tried

but couldn't cry, and then proceed.
You have a stopper and a coded label
for each vial. Are you comfortable?
You should have everything you need.

You see all tears are not the same.
Apply them to the neutral paper
and countless hues appear.
Our study is to give them each a name.

Erato

She is beauty itself and sometimes she likes to leave her home
       where sadness is a music
that guides the moon through noctilucent clouds

and venture downhill through the twisting streets
to where the anger is,
       where new regrets are born.

Sometimes she knows the whole night long that come the morning
she will leave with the empty jug on her head
           (steadied by one hand,
the other on her hip for balance)
       and make her way there;
other times, she just up and goes.

Often when she returns
she finds she has lost a gold hoop from one ear
       which means she will have to go back again.

From an Adirondack Chair

I watched the changing shadows
of clouds the breadth of a reverie
that spanned half a century
moving across green mountains

the scent of mud and grass and
clover just past its bloom joined
in a certain way will always be-
the day that I remembered then

you next to me eyes closed face
toward the sun serene as shadows
moved across us very fast the way
our lives were gathering speed

I Don't Recall Where We Were Going

When we set out, the downpour
was so loud I didn't hear you ask
if we should pull over. I'm sorry.
The child in the backseat followed
a rivulet's path down the window
as if instructive, and the wipers,
struggling to keep up, said life is
luck and love and love and luck and
luck and love as I tried to stay on
the road, torrents pouring across it,
great fans of water slapping us
from gigantic trucks roaring past.
I dared not turn and look at you.
I never was so frightened or alive.

A Marriage

You whom I love most
were reading beneath a tree,
and as I approached,
birds in twos and threes
arrived and filled the branches
until the tree was loud
with twittering, nervous birds
flitting from branch to branch.
Then a thundering of wings,
like a single cry as they departed.
O my love there is more,
much more, still, to know
of love than how to continue.

Vaccine

What is the word for the way
the starling's sheen and the carapace
of the Japanese beetle seem alike?
And if I find it will the dying stop?

Words don't come easily to me.
I used to think they were afraid of me,
they hid in my chest, in my belly.
Will the right ones make the dying stop?

What word is there for the way
some words unsaid erase you?
For our hope not to hurt again?
For what to say to make the dying stop?

Summer Job

"The trouble with intellectuals," Manny, my boss
once told me, "is that they don't know nothing
till they can explain it to themselves. A guy like that,"
he said, "he gets to middle-age — and by the way,
he gets there late; he's trying to be a boy until
he's forty, forty-five, and then you give him five
more years until that craziness peters out, and now
he's almost fifty — a guy like that at last explains
to himself that life is made of time, that time
is what it's all about. Aha! he says. And then
he either blows his brains out, gets religion,
or settles down to some major-league depression.
Make yourself useful. Hand me that three-eighths
torque wrench — no, you moron, the other one."

Doorman

Bright buttons, white gloves, polished shoes,
I kept the glass clean and the brass knobs shining.
A captain's hat and trousers creased and striped,
some tatting on the sleeves, a touch of braid.
It might have been a soldier's uniform.

Over and over, day after day, I opened
the same door for the same rich people
who pretended to think we were equals,
while I, who needed the job to pay rent,
pretended to believe they thought so.

I was so bored it made me happy
to run into the street and blow my silver whistle
then stand there holding the door of a cab
as if I'd just caught a great big fish!
Even if what I do now doesn't matter

as much as I want to think it does, even if
I'm a fool in other ways than I was back then,
I never want to do that kind of work again:
over and over, day after day, opening
the same door for the same rich people.

Near the Library

I heard the bird, then looked to where
it was hidden in the tree's dark center.
I recorded its call with an app on my phone
that captured its rhythm, pitch, and tune —
it's cry, song, warning, whatever it was —
and then identified it by its common name:
A House Finch. Sparrow. Robin. Oriole.
Nightjar. Swallow. Warbler. Ovenbird —
a Mockingbird had fooled the algorithm!
Over and over he sang his repertoire,
a victory for a kind of character I
recognize: I, who love to shelter in
my own dark bower, I, unable to rest,
I, unable to be content with a single song.

Raptor

A silhouette, mostly, in clear October sky.
A goshawk maybe, or a broad-winged,
I'd have to see it again; I can only tell you
I heard its cry and felt its gaze, a laser,
before I passed beneath the aging trees
and kept on, walking and thinking all day.
At dusk the lamps along the path came on,
and lit the leaves a bright unnatural color.
I never knew trees that seemed to worry
so much about what they might say to me
as those along the paved walk out of there:
To be truthful is to remember and grieve.
Then headlights, tail lights, highway, night,
a few clouds passing a half moon, stars.

Formica

I'm eleven. My father hears me say "fuck"
and decides it's time for the talk.
It's my mother's kitchen but she's not there.

I believe he was a little drunk, just loose
not sloppy. He began, several times,
starting over, pulling on a tall brown bottle,

saying my skinny body would pretty
soon change. I watched from far behind
my thank you daddy good boy mask

as he said that men and women fit together
and yes he used his finger and made the O
like OK, sliding in and out. The man's organ,

he used the word *organ*, becomes inflamed,
he used the word *inflamed*, until it spits a
seed inside the woman and that's how babies

come. Do you have any questions son?
He said that it was beautiful, really, as if
he knew he'd failed to make it seem that way.

He said that it was holy. He didn't know
my coach with his crooked *organ* had already
inflamed my pretty body, burned me to ash.

And there and then in that kitchen I froze
what was left of the two of us like cut bait.
Decades gurgled in the pipes below the sink.

The clouds in the tabletop purled like smoke.
On the wall sad Jesus pointed to his heart.
The calendar offered a dozen scenic elsewheres.

Mt. Moriah

A black ant struggled to lug
a crumb a robin dropped
from bread my mother
scattered from the door;
a bee palpated clover blossoms,
somehow like my mother
selecting peaches, or rooting
in the drawer of her vanity
for something discarded.
When I took my father's hand
to switchback up the mountain
of oaths and cutthroat promises
what did we lose? We labored
up the littered, designated trail,
our progress equal to the sum
of all he taught me to ignore.
My father stopped, sighed,
reached down deep in his bag.
"Let's get this over with," he said,
aloud, to no one I could see.

Patrimony

1.

He is out of work.
We are out of money.
My mother's patience
makes him feel worse.
He has lost his temper
again and he is sorry.
Priests have told him
ever since he was a boy
to stop touching himself.
He hides the magazines,
thinks himself weak.
In the doorway of a plane,
you jump, you do not
shake and shit yourself,
kicked into the flak-lit
night the stench of you
like a thing already dead.
It is a long way down.
A lot can go wrong, so
he pretends to know
what a man is, and death;
nothing under his feet
as percussive waves
of light explode around him
like shots of whiskey.
Later he makes believe
he is still the man he
can't remember, the boy
he can't remember.
Maybe there is another
story he was to live.
Maybe he was lazy
and missed his chance.

He wants to be the man
he imagines his wife
loves, the god his father
was to him, the god
he hopes his sons think
him. Complexion: "Ruddy,"
it says on his license.
He loves but still believes
he is pretending.

2.

A son might hold a father
to account for certain
memories, for certain
understandings, to desire
anyone, or anything at all.
A lot can go wrong, so
he pretends to know
what a man is, and love.
He may have to help himself
to his father's shame
for a time to understand.
Sometimes a long time.
And then, even if he turns,
if he rises and bathes
and dresses and shaves
and takes up his life at last,
he cannot say if that is
or is not forgiveness.
The much he must learn
becomes his fate. There is
no might have been, no
otherwise or if only, only
the ground under his feet.
Elsewhere men continue
falling from the sky.

Addict

As a child I saw

faces convulse in disbelief
        and silent mourners
at graveside in black coats quake
     under bowed heads

and couldn't help wanting
        to console us all
    but couldn't

I was only a child
       so I made myself

sick, over and over,
      to have an excuse if ever
        I was asked

if I could remember
       what I thought
     love had charged me to do.

Good Boy

His mother's
chapped lips, flecks
of Lucky
she said *thpt, thpt*
to be rid of,

he cracked, bled
without warning,
held back words,
made himself
a zero,
a portal for smoke.

Shoes

My mother cut holes in her shoes
so her corns would stick out, not
torment her, standing all day
in a mill folding woolen sweaters.

Her shoes stank. They were ugly.
Twin lobsters in a tank at the market,
laces defeated antennae, children
tapping at the glass, saying "Eww."

And she cut linoleum to cover,
from inside, the holes in the soles
because those were the only shoes
she could bear to wear to work

and because she needed to work.
And she soaked her feet in the evening
and smoked and listened to the radio
and dreamed of walking — where?

Chesterfield®

i.m. Dolly Virginia Mattes Hoffman, 1929-1984

Sweat-soaked, a few more moments worth of breath
fought for and won, begged for and granted, you lay back,
relaxed your grip on my hand and made some crack
about how death had scared you half to death
that time and could you have the cool cloth
on your brow, some ice-chips, please, and your black
St. Joseph's Missal? Nobody's fool, the lack
of any hope moved you to reach for faith.
What else could you, or any of us, do?
Three packs a day for years your balm for grief.
(Dad asked me if I thought that he should sue,
as if the law could bring him back his wife.)
I watched you suffer till your death was proof
oblivion is paradise enough.

An Old Story

A few days after my mother died
the furnace went out, and my father,
who had been sitting in his chair
across from hers since the funeral,

his unshaven chin on his chest,
heaved himself up and went down
the cold gray cellar stairs to see if
he could relight the pilot himself

or would have to call for help.
I know what it must have been like
because I remember him other times
on his back down there, cursing

match after match, god damning
each for burning his fingers, as he
reached through the tiny metal door
as many times as it took. This time

it lit, caught, and roared back to life.
When my father sat up he faced
the washer, the dryer, the empty
laundry basket, the ironing board,

and my mother's radio above the sink,
her absence so vivid that climbing
the stairs he thought he heard her
behind him, and he turned around.

Sweat

A man is mowing between the rows of headstones
on a little toy-like tractor. It's hot;
he wipes his face and underneath his cap.
The sun glares off the polished stones.

He hates it - the job, the heat, the flies;
he wanted to be something else.
The sweat on the back of his dark green shirt
could be a black, triangular insignia.

And with his shears, on his hands and knees,
trimming around the crosses, angels, urns,
crawling from stone to stone, he could be
grieving inconsolably for everyone.

Dream of the River

I'd gone to bed drunk again, and so probably
the dream was my body's nightly purification,
its duty to maintain this innocent animal life;
while I thrashed in currents generations deep,
somehow as I was swept away downstream
I was still right there on the shore, beckoning.

If the river was whiskey, I was a divin' duck.

I saw myself there on the riverbank. Of course
it was a dream, of course I was asleep, of course
it was made of the million flashes of sunlight
in sync on the surface, the coupling dragonflies
quick and brittle, the whole dream buzzing loud,
the braided waters green and silver and brown,
and on the riverbank the man I could become
if I would only get things over with and drown.

If the river was whiskey, I was a divin' duck.

Because it was a dream, the river has no name;
no West Branch Big Sorrow River, no Jordan,
maybe because it is altogether made of names,
of all the memories drowned in it, their sounds
a requiem of water over rocks, and some days,
no matter the day and the light, it calls to me.

I would dive down to the bottom, and I would never come up.

Good Will And Salvation

Army clothes well chosen
will camouflage privation
if in fashion and in season,

but better be, among
the well-heeled, on your toes,
and hold your tongue
so nobody ever knows

or suspects your real
origins, your actual class,
or that you got that cool
degree to cover your ass

long before you knew
what it would one day cost,
how it would change you,
what friends would be lost.

Bobber

The two tall boys, brothers, both
with wire-rimmed glasses, with wicker
creels, fly-fishing gear, and vests
with patches of sheepskin shearling
dotted with trout flies, worked their way
downstream in their rubber waders.
When they passed where I sat,
watching my red and white bobber
under a tree limb decorated with
colorful lures, hooks, shiny spoons,
and dangling tangled fishing line,
I felt shame. They might have been
aristocrats, those tall twins. "Hey,"
I waved. "You catching anything?"
They looked at each other, smiled,
and sloshed downstream to the bend.
Or maybe they were a year apart like
my younger brother Bobby and me.
People said we looked like twins.
Once we brought Bobby to fish
from his wheelchair. He caught nothing
and didn't much enjoy himself;
I could tell from the look he gave me,
and from the look he gave me after that
whenever I left the house with my rod.
I envied those fortunate boys their
fancy tackle as I sat there, alone,
with my coffee can of nightcrawlers,
staring at my plastic bobber, wanting
to hurt one or the other of them badly,
and plotting to leave that place forever.

Long Enough

You would have thought it foolish to speak to the dead,
but I have lived two decades longer now than you
and all this time I have carried you in my head

so I think I have the right to question what you said,
dear teacher. My religious upbringing's residue,
you would have thought it, foolish. To speak to the dead,

however, is sometimes necessary, especially haunted
as I am by all the things I know you hoped I'd do
with all this time that I have carried you in my head.

Last night in sleep I followed everywhere you led
until you asked me in a loud voice what I knew.
(You would have thought it foolish to speak to the dead,

but I was dreaming and could not refuse.) I said
that you were wrong, that I could see your bitter view
(since all this time I have carried you in my head)

for what it was, and you for who you were. Instead
of dreaming your reply I woke as you withdrew.
You would have thought it foolish to speak to the dead
but all this time I have carried you in my head.

Dialogue

I went to a nearby cemetery
to speak with some other dead

because the dead are all the same
and laugh that same bitter laughter,

as if my need to understand
why I am alive and my brothers dead

is foolish anywhere, and even if
they knew they wouldn't tell me.

Elegy

i.m. Michael Stephen Hoffman, 1957-1970

Being in us in his new life
is as strange for him
as it is for us to be here

at his grave today
with no one else's footprints in the snow
and only the trees that guided us

so let it not be winter there.

Unearthed

Digging, I struck a small box
and lifted it from the earth.

Inside, coiled, a golden wire,
like a single bronze piano wire.

Freed, it sprung and lashed me,
almost putting out my eye.

I took it home and stretched it
from the lintel to the threshold

and strummed it. Don't ask me
how I knew it was my brother.

It made a sound I remembered.
Not his mutinous-body

but some other part of him,
perhaps the sound for him I made

when our mother first lay him
beside me in our crib, my name

for him before I knew his name.
Now, decades beyond a time

his given name can call him,
I am here with my yearning,

in the doorway, tuning myself
to his thrumming bass note.

Late Elegy

Too young to know better,
my brother and I ate flowers,
pink rose petals; their veins,
I think, convinced us we could,
the thin capillaries in the flesh
of roses heavy on our family's
wicker trellis or hanging over
the neighbors' rickety fence.
We smuggled salt from the kitchen,
sat in the grass, feasted, laughed.
The part of me that might have
remembered what we said was
not yet alive. I only know we
wanted so much to be good
we must have believed we weren't.
One petal at a time, a little salt.
My brother and I ate flowers.

i.m. RJH

This Close

i.m. Robert James Hoffman 1950-1972

Little brother I have forgotten
our secret but I remember
your cupped hand
and steamy breath in my ear

I believe you are near
adjacent
my five hungry senses

with me as if
in the spaces between my fingers

between the letters of my name
between the numbers of my years

in sounds too high for ears
too low for even foot-soles

sometimes I can almost see you
shadow of a helpless fish
in the curl of a breaking wave

or hear you like halyards clinking
on wobbling masts in a foggy harbor

and recently the grieving animal I am
cooked up your likeness in a dream

you recognizably you but nothing

like the way I remember you
your round face intent upon surviving

I never wonder
who you might have become

never think of you as almost

rather as weightless counterweight
as abstract afterward
ungone
a visitor from nowhere

you are
where all the waters go
where I take myself to soothe myself to find a way
to understand your absence

how aging I grew into it
grew onto it like a trellis

Is it your death or mine or ours
or everyone's I am moving through
the whole length of this life you left so early?

They That Mourn

Blessed are they that remember,
for them the muscle of the heart
is twisted as if it is turning away,

or trying to, and what it turns from
is both particle and wave, emitted
from past disaster
but illuminating nothing;

theirs is more than remains.

And blessed are they
that mourn the animals,
that weep for the burning trees,

that roar at the roaring flames
and worry few tears before
were real as these, that turn

the light out, let the night in
and contend with sorrow,

that imagine
what once they are gone
they might wish they had done

and, in that darkness, begin.

Last Hope

If you ever come, my dreamed of world,
the one we almost had, I will be gone
with all the others. After all this waiting
on wooden benches outside in the hall,
after the clicking of heels on polished tile,
after the furious shuffling of papers
and the endless arguments over money,
bring with you people refreshed by love,
disposed to wonder, surprised at cruelty.
Improbable world I once believed in, rising
from words like steam from a bowl of soup,
world like an egg in a nest of the best debris,
if against all odds you take shape one day,
bring people whose hearts are less hesitant,
new people, better people than we were.

New World Order

Heartbreaking breaking news
again, the terse chyron running
across the bottom of the screen

people running across a runway
missing the last plane out last
way to safety last chance to be

a man or woman with a future
a family with enough to eat
a seat on the sofa right here next

to me typing a text to a friend
about another heartbreak
crossing the bottom of the screen

Miracle At Bethany

Why? asked Lazarus.
Why come forth?
Is there peace? Are we now
in the time of justice?

I dream of these things
in the dark, in the earth.
It is my work, brother.
Leave me to it.

Pax Americana

As far as I can tell the empire's still the crucified
as far as the eye can see, hectares of crosses
both sides of the road, their anguish bound
for distribution to the cities and dope-sick towns
that turn to gray stone and enlistment bonuses.

Now rows of solar panels in the stolen fields,
both sides of the road, in a sodden week of rain,
word of another friend's overdosed daughter,
and mine so hurt she can only wail long syllables
trying to tell me what's just happened to her life.

And on the same road, but far from here, trucks
as far as the eye can see hold food and medicine
for refugees and are refused by men well-armed
with crude maps of a future world: this one's
done for, as far as I can tell; it died of cruelty.

As far as I can tell centurions still gamble: who,
in which field, which row, accused of god knows
what, will be first to succumb, and the women
will be forced to carry the war to term again
and be responsible for cleaning it all up afterward.

Everything's like looking through a dirty window,
no let up in sight the rain not washing anything.
Soldiers turn children to meat and bloody rags,
take off their helmets and, thumbs up, snap a selfie
that ends up in a magazine about investments.

On both sides of the road there are walls going up
that at home in the empire most are grateful for
since what is done with our tribute hurts to hear:
high tension lines from the fields of crosses hum,
and echoing hammers ring, building god knows what.

Fruit in Season

That spring after my brother's death
I worked in an orchard. Young, good
with a ladder, I pruned apple trees,
lopped crossed limbs, nipped spurs,
and comforted myself with the notion
my brother was busy underground
carefully disentangling the long roots,
season after season, tree by tree;
but now I know there are people
who tread the earth like water
because below them their dead
are trying to grasp their ankles
and pull them under, so I know
how lucky I am and how grateful
I ought to be: sick for long years
my brother begrudged me nothing.

Trapdoor

Grief is the floor.
      There is a door there,

          a door in the floor:

      on the other side,
on the underside, in the dark,

      along with pipes and wires, is what
          rests
      on what, what now
          and again shifts,
        settles,
shears.

        I miss my brothers.

In Memoriam

Shadows, they remain
inside the outline of my shadow always
as per our agreement,
their abiding cool desire,
and the laws of light.
I have sometimes stayed with them
all night in the dark
when we can be most ourselves
together.

If they had a word
for when the sun rises
it would be the same as our word
for remembering,
and because we are never really apart
we call it mine,
this time since their deaths,

as if time must belong to someone,
as if I were not a shadow too,
as if we were not all
the sun's
misshapen children.

Cold Requiem

Tonight the harbor is the sea: waves
thunder, detonate on rocks, slosh
over the seawall. The glaring moon
has dissolved the stars.
Few others are out, it is so cold.

If I walk to the end of the pier
in this eye-watering wind, boards shuddering
under me, might I find what to say
to my friends, mourning their daughter?

If this night has any advice,
it's in a language I don't understand.

My children are alive and healthy.
How can my words not hurt?

The question is a cloud of breath.

A Good While

I thought of the time I sliced my thumb and how, even there,
     where the nerve endings are most acute, where the sensitivity
          resides that, touched by each finger in turn, made us human,
demanded that the ganglions of the head learn to cooperate
     and grow, and count, and speak, even there with the little cap
          and piece of nail sliced off, for a good while I felt nothing
but regret: oh shit, why'd I go and do that? No pain. Not yet. And I thought
     then maybe a frightened soldier, hit by a bullet, might just die
          before the pain could start, feeling suddenly woozy, sleepy,
thinking, shit: I'm hit, blood pressure dropping fast, dizzy and
     darkening, maybe saying to himself oh boy I hope this isn't dying,
          and I prayed, especially for the sake of my neighbor's son,
that that is more or less the way it happens.

Headache Clinic

tortures are just what they were, only the earth has shrunk
and whatever goes on sounds as if it's just a room away.
—Wislawa Szymborska

Yes, the pain is worse since last time I was here;
I've tried to become accustomed to it. Last night
while I was trying to find a comfortable position
and wondering if I should take a pill,
a man a couple of miles from here came home,
walked quietly upstairs, took out his gun,
and murdered his wife and two children,
a boy and a girl, while they slept.
The paper had photos. He shot himself too.
A fourteen year old's parents want to know
who duct-taped the bombs to his hairless chest
under the Warner Bros. T-shirt his uncle
brought him with a cap from Florida last year.
Doctor, when you shine that penlight in my eyes,
do you see the man take off his shoes inside the door
so as not to wake his sleeping wife and kids?
You want me to point to the part of my head that hurts?
That's it, that part. I can follow your finger, yes,
from where the boy left the small repair garage,
past the tented book-stall and the cashew vendors,
to where he entered the crowded restaurant.
Do you see her? The woman, her finger in the air,
who has just caught the eye of the waiter?
On a scale of 1 to 10, your pen in hand, you ask,
"How badly does it hurt right now?"

Photos of Gaza: November, 2024

I felt sure I was closing in on something
to say, clear and beyond all argument,
when I saw a child mashed to a paste,
the shredded meat of her mocking words.

I have nothing to say not evident
to anyone with eyes, with a stomach
that churns with revulsion, with ears
for cries that encompass every language.

I am no longer bewildered by cruelty,
have not been speechless facing suffering,
but I have nothing now to say to anyone
to move them to change their minds.

I am not offering this poem for judgment.
I am not trying to win a poetry prize.
I am trying to continue to love my kind
in the face of shamelessness and slaughter.

"So What"

Here is a tiny weapon, devastating, undetectable.
Here is the switch to turn off the world.

The demise of an ancient question;
the voice no longer rises,

and a black hole, antimatter, widens
like a desperate pupil in the sudden dark.

The Road

Mothers with newborns in knotted slings,
on their heads impossible towers of things,

      the old in carts, the children by the hand,
      these people crossing a cratered land

          are more than metaphor;
                but they are also metaphor.

We are the truth to one another. Look:
don't wait for some historian's book

      to understand this (then it will be too late.)
      This is the unchecked power of the State,

          the end of empathy, the rise of Mars,
                the avarice that in the end mars

all our laws and medicine and art.
Show me one fleeing person's heart

      and I will show you a thousand griefs
      for loves, hopes, memories, beliefs

          that war has undermined.
                Corpses plowed under, mined

roads and fields, the groves and orchards
poisoned, fathers and brothers tortured,

      hope abandoned with the other heavy furniture —
      it isn't much of a road, the future,

          if you don't know where
                it goes or it goes nowhere.

Corollary

The body,
six feet
underground,

takes six days
to begin
to break down.

Bulbs must wait
in warming loam
six months

or more. And so
the earth is vast,
love urgent.

O

There is a moment of such pain,
beside an open grave,
when someone must hold you up,

when the only difference that matters
is between the living and the dead:

Could we remember, O,
what hatred could survive?

To An Embryonic Stem Cell

Alphabet. Mockingbird. Skeleton key.
Stoical, stock-still, sharp-eyed lifeguard.
"With no desire or hatred in your heart,
there is no need to show off or pretend."*
Soul of generosity, how do you do
it, follow the oftentimes ambiguous,
occasionally erring path the body's
syntax ought to have, among a clutch
of inborn or environmental
choices, made, hone in, and find
where meaning failed, that break,
and fix it? Blank stare, I can see you
there on the bench in the bullpen,
cap pulled down, not signing autographs,
smelling like a brand new box of crayons,
neat as a shrink wrapped deck of cards.
Sworn friend. Trickster. Tikkun's angel.
Oblate. Virtuoso. Smooth-cheeked Virgo.
Shaman. Seamus. Speck of spirit.
Eligible, agreeable, truest love.
Divulge your secrets, phoenix fire!
O protein protean and pluripotent,
teach us how to mend our selfish lives.

* Milarepa

Déjà Vu

As if a bird
alighted
on a mirror
a moment
and then was gone

(the name

"vireo"

arising
as the image
of the bird
rose
to the bird
but
more slowly)

so, from deep,

grief

is known
afterward,

when even a single
instant
matches it.

A Letter to Walt Whitman in the Earth

Walt, under my boot-soles
you smell like naphthalene and paint
whenever the water table rises, and no one
is held accountable. You were irascible
post-stroke, talked bigotry
that marred the glory of your work,
a mite infected eagle come to earth,
clumsy, ripping the neighborhood garbage bags.
But I need your *Homo sum...*, your orchestral *acapella*,
singing of us already in my great grandfather's time.
Now generalists with cell phones selling wellness
on the beltways of America at eighty mph believe
they are the first to want a life that's more than labor
and have made that aim a creed. They pray: *May I get mine.*
Your beautiful *roughs* are trained to kill,
contractors now, not *camerados*,
and none are heard above the mating calls
of money sounding in the air instead of the flocks
of sparrows you heard in Camden. Do I sound bitter?
Very well then, I am bitter. I am large. I contain
our entire betrayal, Walt — caged children, murdered
citizens, poisoned water, spent uranium — by those
for whom democracy's an obstacle and humans
resources. And it's hard to feel amative, loafing here,
my soul so far declining my invitation, maybe
because a surveillance cam has noted me, a kosmos,
and is now uploading my worried face and stats
to a gleaming satellite in orbit high above These States.

Of Thee

My country wonders at the looks it gets.
It likes to hang around the Army/Navy store,
admiring this uniform and that insignia,
badges and big blocky numbers for everyone,
singing "Take Me Out to the Ballgame" off-key.
It is always looking in the gutters for money.
With a gun from its collection, it shot itself
right smack in the history. It can't remember.
Something's been stolen but it can't say what.
It can't remember, so everything happens now.
It likes to hang around the Army/Navy store,
admiring this uniform and that insignia,
badges and big blocky numbers for everyone,
singing "Take Me Out to the Ballgame" off-key.

Betrayal

One's-self I sing, a simple separate person
— Whitman

Earth's tragicomic bricolage,
        I am imagined

of necessity and desire — oh,
and fear; mustn't forget fear.

So I see angels
jutting from corbels and cornices,
their appearance

                suggested by air conditioners
                high above the avenues

        as the planet
reaches combustion temperature
        and a bit of friction here or there
                burns down a city

of people reading, playing, cooking, sleeping,
sharing their innocent puzzlement,

telling one another their neighborly lies.

        Shrieking mirror
        neurons split the atoms
belonging to me, belonging to you, and

corruption runs in the gutters
        and celebrates itself,
laughing and only mildly ashamed.

Now everyone can see the future
        as if possessed
of powers they never had before,
            though most refuse.

My country, 'tis
        a giant clock
above a loud arena of applauding victims,
        and children without the choice
                not to believe.

Messengers

The house itself, if it had a voice
Would speak out clearly. As for me,
I speak to those who understand;
if they fail, memories are nothing.
                        — Aeschylus, *Agamemnon*

We say what we know because we must.
You can cheer us or run us out of town.
It's nothing at first, like rain on dust,

a hairline crack in the faultline's crust,
a tentative first-person plural pronoun.
We say what we know because we must

recall, recount, redeem, and readjust
all that we've known, not for renown.
It's nothing at first, like rain on dust,

or the first few tiny flecks of rust
on barrels buried underground.
We say what we know because we must

talk back to histories we do not trust,
relearn our own, and set them down.
It's nothing at first, like rain on dust.

What does it mean to fear what's just?
You can cheer us or run us out of town.
We say what we know because we must.
It's nothing at first, like rain on dust.

Founders' Gallery

This old man, he play one,
he play walk like I walk, son.
With a six-pack, heart-attack,
leave me all alone,
this old man come rolling home.

This old man, he play two,
he play Listen I know you.
With a back-slap, wise-crack,
cut me to the bone,
this old man drove me from home.

This old man, he play three,
he play don't talk back to me.
With an Abraham and Isaac,
change to baritone,
this old man afflict his home.

This old man, he play four,
he play imitation lore.
With a gimcrack, bronze plaque,
soldier's tomb unknown,
this old man forgot his home.

This old man, he play five,
he play let's see you survive.
With a headwhack, flashback,
manmade danger zone,
this old man oppress his home.

This old man, he play six,
he play world is made of pricks.
With a greenback, smokestack,
no one else can own,
this old man he sold my home.

This old man, he play seven,
he play eight by tens of heaven.
With a Kodak, Cadillac,
turkey's dry wishbone,
this old man lured me from home.

This old man, he play eight,
he play duck and obfuscate.
With a brainwrack, sidetrack,
who he is unknown,
this old man pretend he's home.

This old man, he play nine,
he play everything just fine.
With a handclap, laughtrack,
telephone postpone,
this old man believes he's home.

This old man, he play ten,
he play Rex Coelestis, men.
With an ack-ack, nightflack,
flashbulb hecatomb,
this old man destroys our home.

Monument

Should there be
a memorial, a stone

inscribed
To Those Who Resisted,

let it not be placed
in the square
renamed so many times,

nor in the park
where the poor seek shelter,

nor the busy plaza.

Should there be
a memorial, build it

deep in a forest,
high on a mountain,

requiring one to be
a pilgrim, perhaps

on a rock in the harbor;
no, in the heart,

yes, in the heart,
a stone in the heart.

Good Friday

He's gone
to find the animal
who tells the story
that destroys us;
he wants to interview
the angel with the teeth;

unearth
disfigured miniature
intaglios: clay
dolls of heroes, words
burnt into buried stones,
the molds for masks we

memorized
and wear for worship,
somber and nodding and
simpler than we know we are.
Look at the bloodless body
hanging from a rootless tree:

no wonder
in our fear we carve it,
paint it, sing of it, and
pray to believe that only one
unlike ourselves is sanctioned
to attempt such things.

The One

*Lockheed Martin, Boeing, Raytheon, General Dynamics,
Northrup Grumman, Honeywell, RTX Corporation,
L3Harris Technologies...*

I'm only the pen in the pocket
protector of the manager who
signed off on the pallet of kits
sent to assembly. I'm only one
diode to be spot soldered to a
green motherboard, passed to
the next assembler on the line.
I am one single drop of solder,
to be placed in the same place
in exactly the same place each
time while never given a plan
or even the name for what I'm
part of only the parenthetical
stamps when I arrive or leave.
I am one beep in the beeping
as the forklift crosses painted
lines on the gray cement floor.
I'm one checkmark in one box,
one shift, one task, one break,
one family, one paystub. One.
I am not the one responsible.

At CVS: Aisle 4, Magazines

Some people paid some other people
some money to write some things so that
some other people would pay some money
to read what those people wrote so that

the people who had paid for the people
to write those things would be paid back
with interest so they'd have more money
to pay new people to write the same things;

so naturally as time went on some words,
the names of some other things, vanished,
and, little by little, but accelerating, those
things the unbought words referred to

died, and what was called reading finally
became a bright and vacuumed place where
censorship was unheard of, and everyone
read whatever people were paid to write.

An American Boyhood

My toy gun looked just like the gun my father carried in the war. It
looked like the guns on TV. I learned to make the sound of gunfire with
my mouth. No one made the sound of a ricocheting bullet better: a loud
plosive followed by a little whistle, diminuendo. I spent a lot of time
in my fantasy world, drawing on bad guys, pivoting and crouching.
I holstered my gun. Drew it again. When I got bored, I sat on a swing
and wondered where everybody else was. I did all these things. If you
had an American boyhood, so did you. Tamir Rice had an American
boyhood; his was a Black one, a short one.

D(r)one

What was done was done
in our names; we ourselves

would never have done
what was done to anyone.

We wanted to be good,
polite, obedient, fun,

wanted only not to need
to ask *What have we done?*

And yet, in our names,
what was done was done.

Refugee

A man carries his door,
the door of his house,
because when the war is over
he is going home

where he will hang it
on its hinges
and lock it, tight,
while he tries to remember
the word for welcome.

If his house is gone
when he returns,
he will raise it from rubble
around this door.

If he cannot return,
the door will remember
the rest of the house
so he can build it
again, elsewhere.

And if he cannot go on,
his door can be a pallet
for his rest, a stretcher
to carry him, his shade
from sun, his shield.

Aftermath

(Bosnia, 1996)

for Sara Terry

A trout on a river-bank
knows where the river is;

a fox in a trap
knows the time,

but a man or woman
only knows the story

hope tells, or fear,
and often chooses wrong.

No ant will enter
another's hill,

no bee another's hive,
and a rook, atop

a dead oak,
knows which side it's on,

but a man or woman,
led by liars,

will discuss, calmly,
who should dig the pit

and if it is a better
lesson to slaughter

the neighbors' babies

first or afterward.

A squirrel burrows deep
in a hollow trunk;

the bear returns
to her darkened cave,

but a man or woman,
gorged on blood,

deep in history, asleep,
dreams peace

and waking, says
peace is a dream.

A rabbit may cower,
but only so long;

the common sparrow
knows the seasons,

but a man or woman
only wants a song, a poem,

a religion to profess
that no one who has known

goodness even once
is ever wholly lost.

Without Wings

for Swanee Hunt

In the cemetery,
women of stone, read
books of what is done
and cannot be changed.
Not far away, women
are carrying handbags,
as if shopping, along rows
of unearthed remains
in the high school gym.
They have hurried past
the empty pedestal
in the sniper's sights,
crawled from blasted buses,
lied, dissembled, hidden
the fugitive, given
the refugee a warm
loaf for the journey,
slipped past checkpoints
and remembered
where each tree, gate,
garden used to be,
and in which books
the words are written
that tell, despite what
has been done, what
must be done.

Refusal

Go away, angel,
why would I wrestle?

I have lost every time
I said yes. This time

the answer's "no."
Go away, angel, go.

Gaza Aftermath (2021)

for Mosab Abu Toha

Shalt not yeah not kill but come on hella money.
Fires in the street drones in the air a love poem
speared and flapping on a crooked pike of rebar.

Death, listen, for your own good stop consorting
with murderers, it gives the wrong impression.
We owe you after all, and all of us are good for it.

Before the first door opened with old designs
the story of it all was right there in the book—
how fear becomes hatred—if you read it right.

I used to think we are here to help one another
believe all this is real and sometimes beautiful.
I only think that sometimes now. Which words

at least won't make things worse? Which stars
are stars and which surveillance satellites?
Remember, there are two sides to every dollar.

An elegy claws its way up grief's hoarse throat,
a dirge that could fracture your ribcage calling
to a world where such singing might bring peace.

In the rubble a child's remains are unearthed
right there, dead center in our future, and a photo
goes viral as in vain we mumble ancient poems.

The weight of dread is no lighter when shared.
Barbed wire rusts but razor wire just gleams.
You can change a map; a calendar is different.

After Guernica

we believed we'd seen it and seen it
clearly: sociopathy and its rationale,

the need of the state, protection racket
that gives the bullies not only something

to do, but something to do without
account, with impunity. Over the door

not the blood of the lamb but the word
WAR: so that now in that house death

is welcome, invited, as in Gaza,
where two men hold a dead child

for the camera, for our eyes.
Pity? Yes. Horror? Yes.

Who cares what we feel, looking?
We retch at the wretched. Who

are not us. We are troubled at
the breakdown of diplomacy.

Negotiations have broken off.
Yes, right there: where the child's foot

once was, there, where, like a leg
of lamb, the bone pokes through.

Caesar

Arriving at the podium on the tarmac,
he stands up tall and makes a big fuss
rolling up his sleeves like drawing back

his foreskin, and only amnesiacs
still traumatized and children
do not know what happens next.

On Being Asked to Write a Poem
on the Theme of Liberation

I wish I understood what liberation is,
but history seems to come down to this:
behind us cut sod and a mound of soil,

a trench of jerky and bone, each skull
stained and broken, an empty husk.
Our truck gasps and grinds as dusk

shifts day's hoarse gears a second time,
a dismal sound that will forever rhyme
with respite but never catharsis.

I wish I understood what liberation is.
I looked for something I could quote,
but Ecclesiastes reads like a suicide note,

and cheap grace, as the martyred Pastor
Bonhoeffer called it, that instant Easter
resurrecting victims and perps alike,

is our most cowardly mistake:
after such knowledge, what? What?
Don't. Don't speak the word. To liberate

our children's children's children,
maybe, provide them with an antigen
of an idea, maybe we can manage that

if we begin right now to search for it,
no salve, but a vaccine against malice,
so they might know what liberation is.

An Emblem From Dresden

In Rembrandt's *The Rape of Ganymede*[2]
        the boy, a chubby toddler torn from his play,
                kicks and wails and pisses in terror as,

clamped in beak and talon, he looks down.
        The sky is smoke, a billowing smudge
                as after the city's bombardment.

The eagle is unnatural, painted in the way
        myth borrows nature for its purposes,
                larger and more saurian, power from on high,

but the boy, as Rembrandt understood, is real
        and not especially beautiful, a fat boy fed
                the diet of the poor: potatoes, turnips, bread,

and for sweetness the cherries in his fist.
        Ovid has Orpheus sing the story Hermes,
                the slippery consigliere, tells the parents:

the boy will learn the language of the mighty,
        an acolyte, loved and provided for, a story
                that comes with a payment of valuable horses,

wealth enough to secure the future, more
        than even a grown son could expect to earn
                them. What does the boy see, rising? Over Laos

200,000 children trafficked into Thailand's
        brothels, building sites, and sweatshops; over
                Kazahkstan, Uzbekistan, Afghanistan, Albania,

---

2. 1635, Oil on canvas, 171 x 130 cm, Gemäldegalerie, Dresden.

procurers riding shotgun, helicopter cargo
      bound for prostitution in the streets of Athens;
            from Nigeria, bush pilots make the short flight

over jungle to the secret auction, "Clean, no HIV. No HIV."
      Euros for their trouble from the French, the Belgians;
            dollars from Americans.[3] The eagle on the money,

each child a disappearance. "Too young," says the madam,
      pulling back the beaded curtain for her client,
            "no boom-boom this one, not yet, only yum-yum."

3. US Dept of State, Human Rights Report, 1999; ECPAT International, "A Step Forward" 1999; and UNICEF, "State of the World's Children" 1997.

Decorated

When we were boys you
palmed my ten year old head
and held me underwater
for so long parts of me
are thrashing down there still.

So now a photograph of you,
a bald old man like me
smiling with a grandchild on your lap
unsettles me, especially
with all those medals on your chest.

For a Slain Poet

i.m. Hashem Shaabani

Your killers drew the zipper across the black bag like
the sign friends made across their mouths
when you opened yours in the wrong company

        and carried you out of there.

Kings, we all know, build palaces,
hoard riches, gather armies of impoverished
and fierce young men, and make war.

But a king who will kill a poet out of fear?
There remains no evil on earth he will not do.

You, however, who have reminded us
of the truth of the lovers we are, you are
already in paradise

where, solely for your pleasure,
the one god has bestowed upon you seventy-two
blank pages
and your favorite pen,

along with a whole new alphabet
made from the shadows of birds in flight,

the flash of ripples on the lake in sunlight,

letters in the shapes of the many intersecting shadows of the grass,

and the sheen of blown sand, sheared from the crest
of a shifting dune by the Khamaseen,

marks to represent the sound of weeping,
signs for the sound of laughter,

but nothing too clear, none of them
just right, nowhere the once-and-for-all expression

that would obliterate desire. If I thought
what you wanted was rest, if any of your poems
could be so construed, I would wish you rest.

Top of the Hour

There's something about gold
in the American River on the news.
Standing on the bank, on TV, deep
in El Dorado County California,
a woman explains to a reporter
that the river is hope for some,
for others erosion everywhere
has already left them nothing
but river rocks knocking together.
Prodigious winter rainfall and
snow have exposed deposits.
Once there was business on Main
besides prospectors' shops. Now
no one trusts anyone anymore.

Go

Once walking in a town I was told
was dead center of the continent,
I saw a man on a bicycle stopped at
an intersection, traffic light swinging
in the wind off the plains. A Sunday
afternoon redlight, no cars for miles.
Crossing, I flashed him a brief wave.
He kept squinting at the traffic signal.
A block and a half on, I looked back
and there he was — for all we know
he could be there now, still waiting
to go left, or right, or straight ahead.
I walked farther in the wind, knowing
history and worrying for my children.

Dusk

I will die in Paris in a rainstorm, on a day I already remember.
—Cesar Vallejo
(tr. Andres Rojas)

Whether or not there is a river,
I will be by a river. My mother
will send my father to fetch me.
He will toot the horn twice and I
will wish for more time. As usual,
I've caught nothing. And whether
or not I have already given up,
I will know I have to go. I will
put my gear in the trunk. *Whump.*
He will lean across the front seat
and swing open the door, and I
will enter the musk of the car,
the smoky sweat of my father,
and note the regret on his face.
Though I was not always glad
to see him, I am glad to see him.
Whether or not I want more time,
the sky will continue darkening.
Already there are stars, and waist
high at the wood's edge, fireflies.
My father clutches and shifts,
then touches me on the shoulder,
staring ahead, eyes on the road.

Night Walk

The mouse in silver grass, ears cocked
for the whir of wings, notes the owl

has left its branch, while clouds occlude
and then allow the perilous moon.

Shall I ask the marmot for advice,
The quick bats what to do?

The trees appear aluminum in moonlight.
Tomorrow will tell what was done.

Lower Piney Creek, Banner, WY

The creek brightly gargling over knocking rocks,
      time tumbling in several speeds at once.

An undulant trout like a windsock in the current
      caught me noticing and disappeared.

That we glimpse one another at all is a miracle;
      the mountains are no more than dunes.

A fly on my hand investigates the creases in my skin,
      assessing me, how long until I'm food?

Light off the water leaves a white spot in my vision,
      dark against red when I close my eyes.

Hatteras, Sunset

Breakers boom on the sand.
A gull tumbles in a crosswind,

rights himself, then glides
in oblique and waning light.

What does what I want
have to do with anything here?

What is is, and also its brief
moving shadow, *was.*

Still Life

To the man before the picture, his heart
is that soft pheasant spilling from the table
among the grapes, the glass decanter,
and the silks that evince the painter's skill;

but more likely the truth is elsewhere:
who can claim to see his own heart clearly
and still be trusted? And just because a man
believes his heart can't rise again and fly

does not ensure that someone like you
won't walk, distracted, into the gallery,
and, unnoticed by anyone else, knock over
the wine that will forever stain everything.

Cove

Small waves repeat,
sink into sand,
an escalator, down.

Soft flesh in a broken
shell. Tangled rope.
Stones worn human.

I forgot what
I meant. I forgot
what I meant to say.

Terms Of Occupancy

In heaven you must promise
never to forget
you are in heaven.

In hell you must promise
never to forget
to want to be elsewhere.

On earth you must promise
never to forget
there are no promises.

In Hora Mortis Nostrae

1.

To say the day
of my unpersoning
nears is wrong,

as blue sky is
untrue although
a truism,

a prism of gas
and sunlight,
(neuron and word)

"alas" is
an idea
way too small;

2.

better the blue
and beatific
Maria, Mater,

balanced, calm
acrobat atop
all, crushing

the poison snake
in childhood's
dark church,

just the way that
cloud, changing
as the face

of my dying
mother, has nothing
to do with fear.

"Fantastic Voyage"

1.

Like one of the characters from that old matinee, I am inside the heart
but somehow it is my own heart and I am inside a humming room, waiting

before a round door I know to be a valve that will admit a flood of the past,
a forceful torrent of what is depleted, the valve like a spaceship's airlock,

and before I open it I must unlock the corresponding valve in the far wall,
which I understand is the future, and stand back, or history will drown me.

2.

There are these griefs, you see, starved, desiccated as the tiny corpses
of insects left in abandoned webs that quiver with my movements

here in this creaky attic or cellar, someplace I don't visit often
enough to recognize the things I have piled there haphazardly.

Anything of worth I find here I find looking for something else
among the things I chose to store away for some other, easier life.

3.

Inside me are places where conclusions and confessions are conjecture
because the dead have left behind them a film of sticky shame

and a granulated record of deeds and misdeeds like the residue of sleep
around the eyes each morning. *Merrily, merrily, merrily, merrily* I pull

the cord to try to start the engine but my little boat drifts downstream
toward the falls highlighted on the map. Maybe it won't be so bad.

Inventory

What I have given to sorrow,
though I have poured out
all I am again and again,
does not amount to much.

One winter's snows.
Two loves I could not welcome.
A year of mostly silence.
Another man I might have been.

Instructions

Say I was filled with regret
because I always fell for the future,
and that I learned that hope, like the rain,
can make the wrong things grow.
Explain I would have mourned
much longer if the world had let me.
Say that I hope to be remembered,
and that I wish I had forgotten less.

Set right the rumor I was ever
a believer: a story was told to me
as knowledge and I loved it once,
an arrangement of premises on which
I learned to build all you recall of me.
Belief has nothing to do with faith.
The first I lost early and all at once,
the second later, one loss at a time.

Tell them that, a sailor, I knew fog
was no excuse and certainly no comfort.
Assure them that when I had nothing
to say I said nothing, kept still,
and let things come clear in their time.
Because I spoke clearly does not mean
I remained unlettered, simple, or naïve:
tell them I saw all there was to see.

Acknowledgments

The author wishes to thank the editors of the following magazines in which many of the new poems have appeared, sometimes in a slightly different version:

Hudson Review, Ibbetson Street, Lily Poetry Review, The Manhattan Review, New World Writing, Pangyrus, Plume, Soundings East, Vox Populi, Woven Tale Press

A special thanks to my editor, Eileen Cleary. Thanks also to Kathleen Aguero, Richard Cambridge, Lee Hope, Tom Mallouk, Dennis Nurkse, J. D. Scrimgeour, and the late Baron Wormser for their critical readings of several of these poems, which are the better for their suggestions.

About the Author

Richard Hoffman has published five books of poetry, *Without Paradise; Gold Star Road*, winner of the Barrow Street Press Poetry Prize and the Sheila Motton Award from The New England Poetry Club*; Emblem*; *Noon until Night*, winner of the 2018 Massachusetts Book Award, and his most recent, *People Once Real*. His other books include *Half the House: a Memoir*; the 2014 memoir *Love & Fury*; the story collection *Interference and Other Stories*, and the essay collection *Remembering the Alchemists*. His work, both prose and verse, appears in such journals as *Agni, Consequence, Harvard Review, Hudson Review, The Literary Review, The Manhattan Review, PN Review (UK), Poetry, Witness, World Literature Today* and elsewhere. He is Emeritus Writer in Residence at Emerson College in Boston, and nonfiction editor of *Solstice: A Magazine of Diverse Voices*.